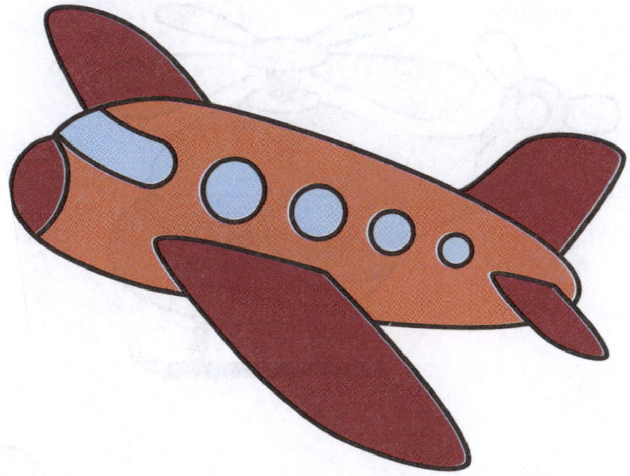

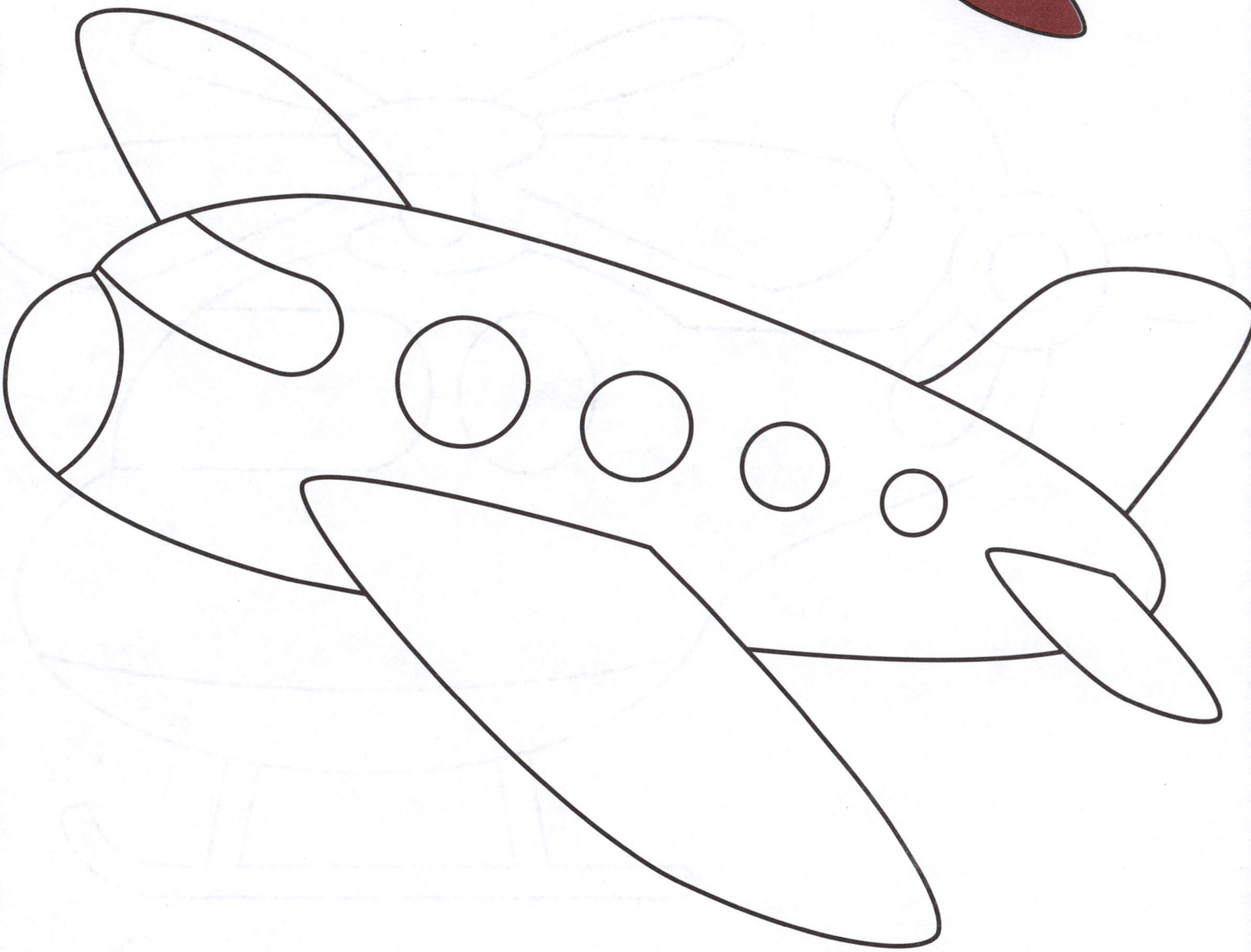

aircraft

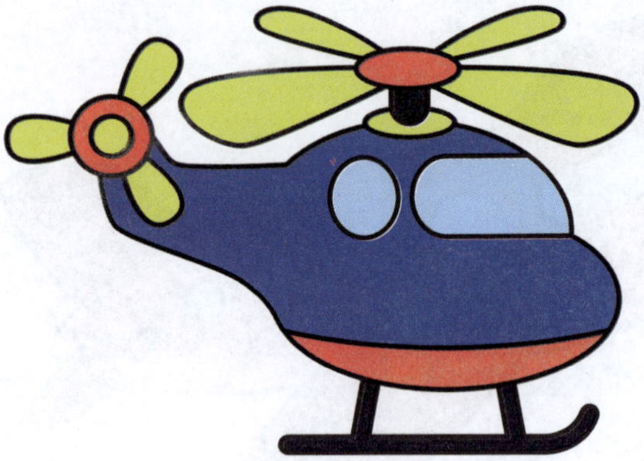

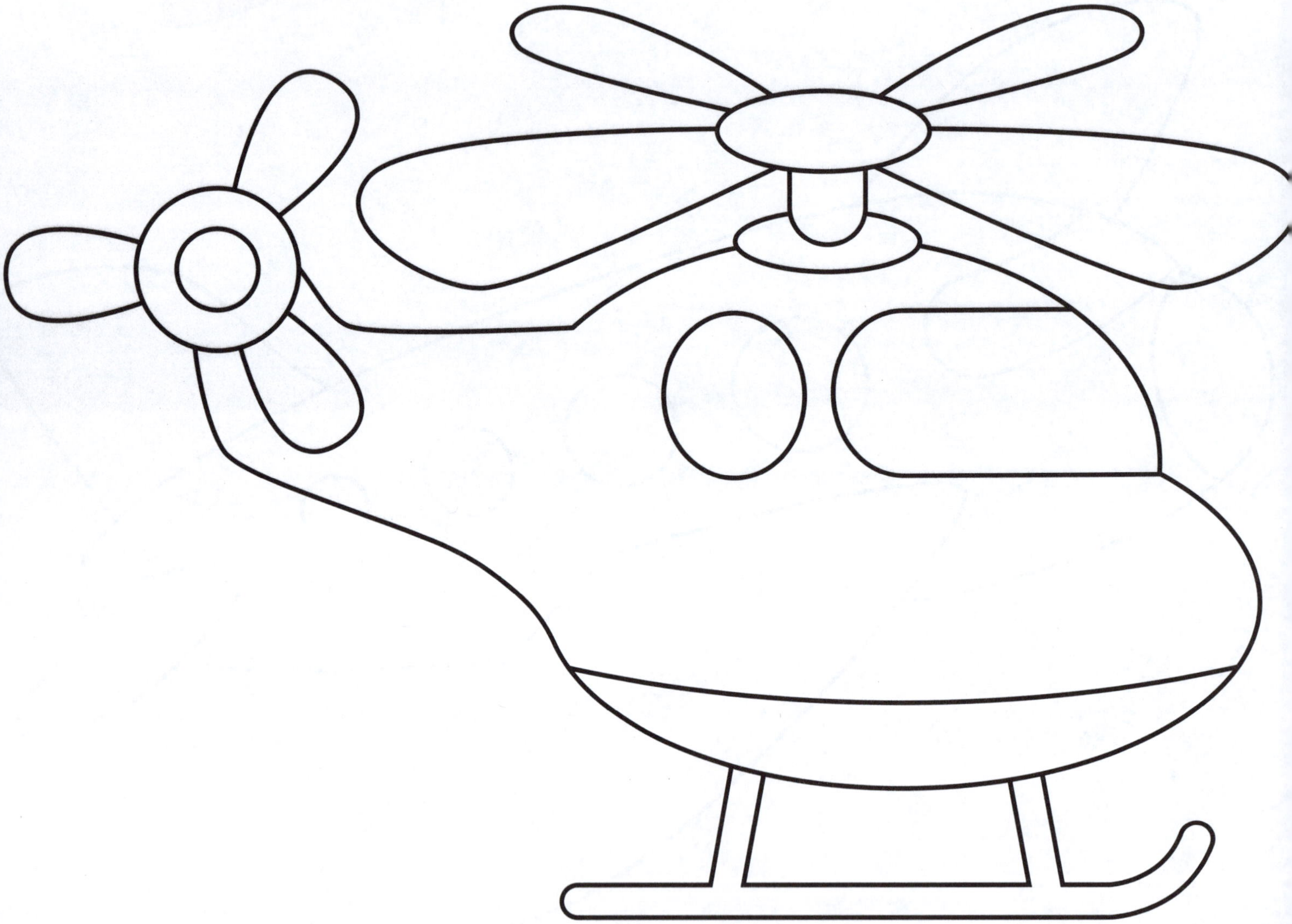

helicopter

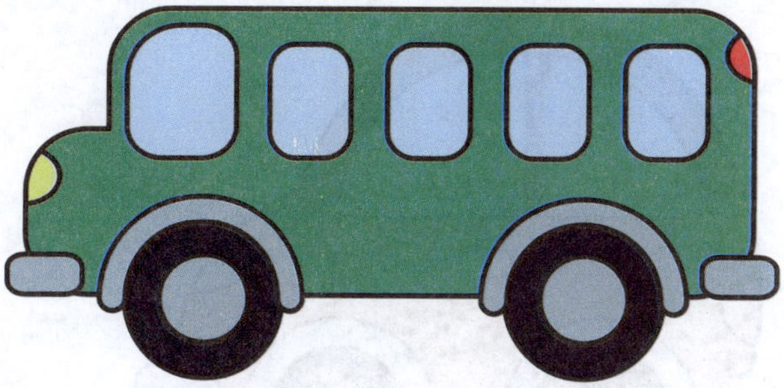

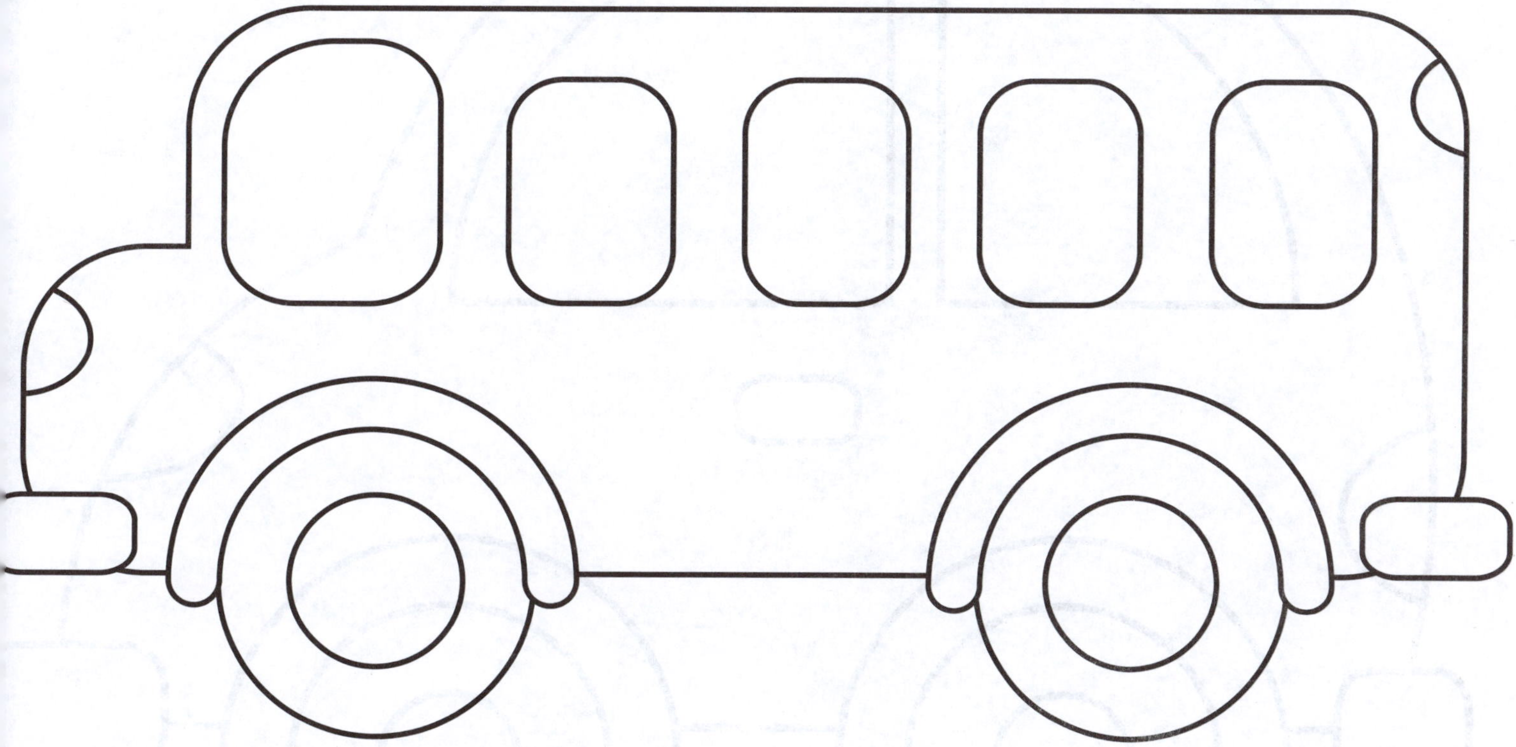

bus

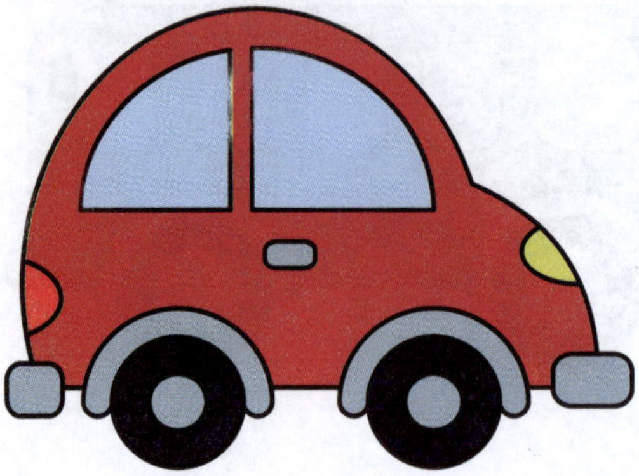

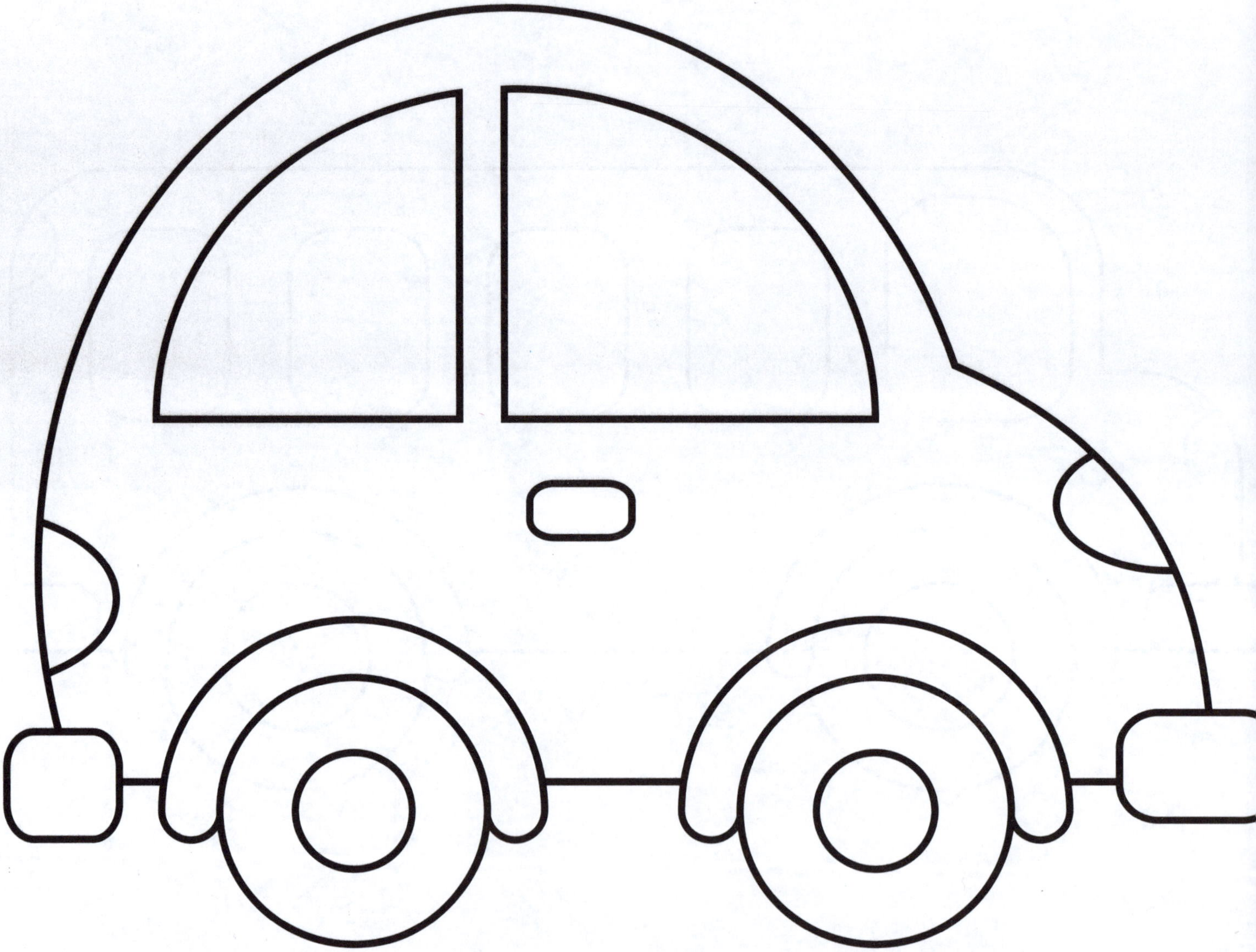

car

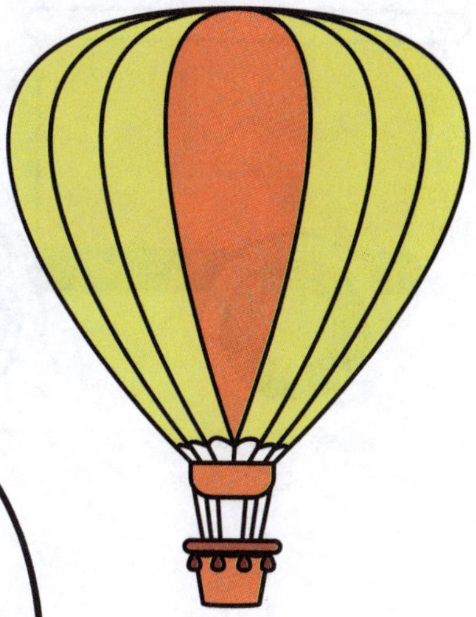

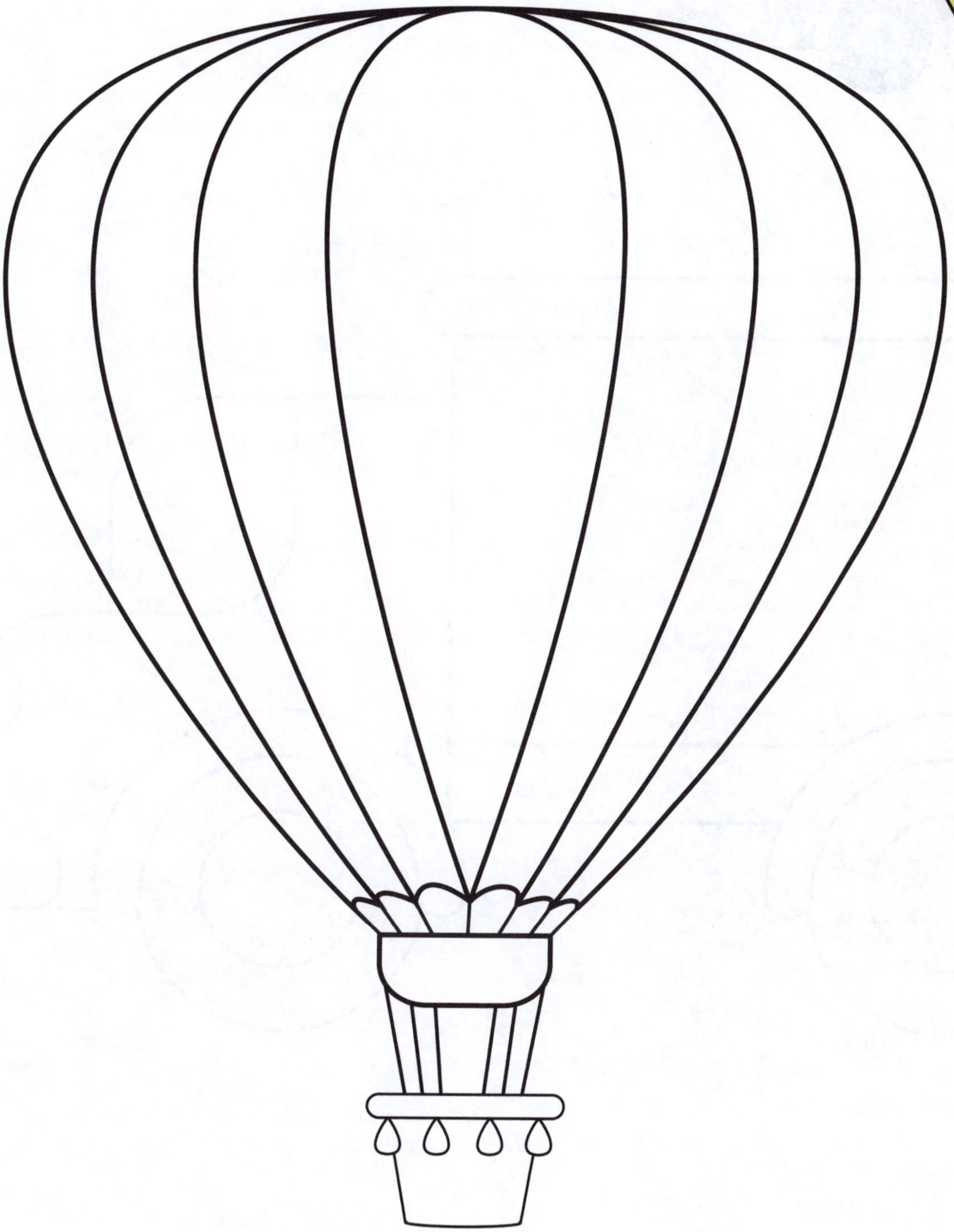

hot air balloon

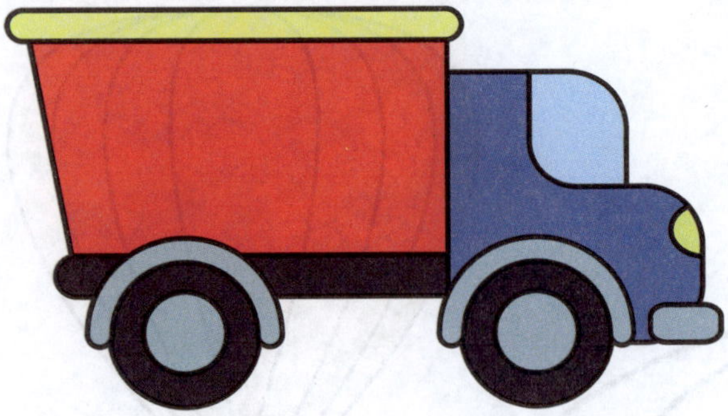

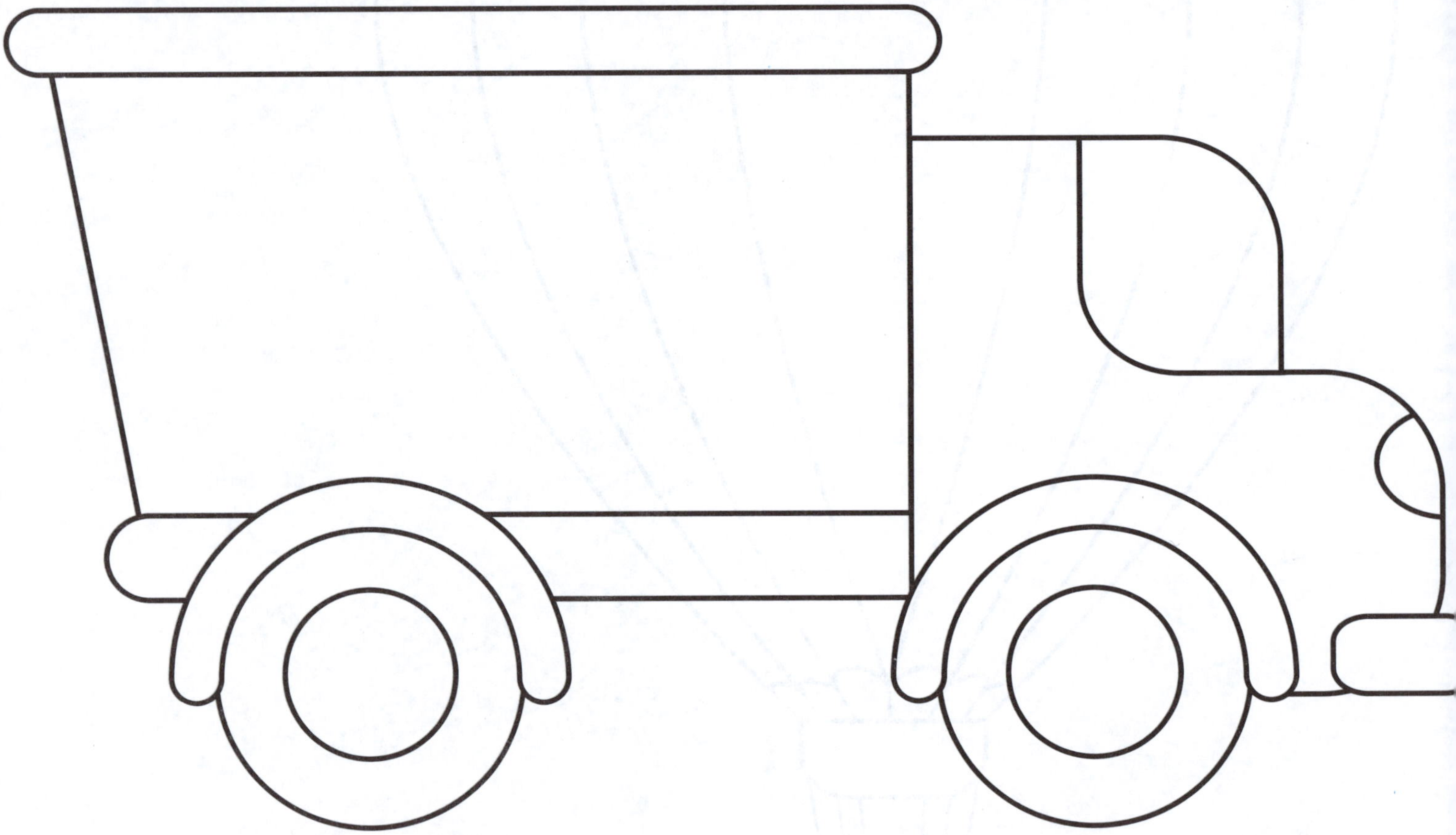

truck

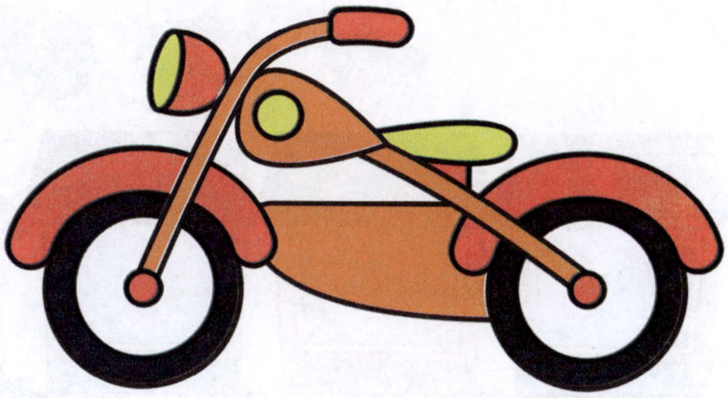

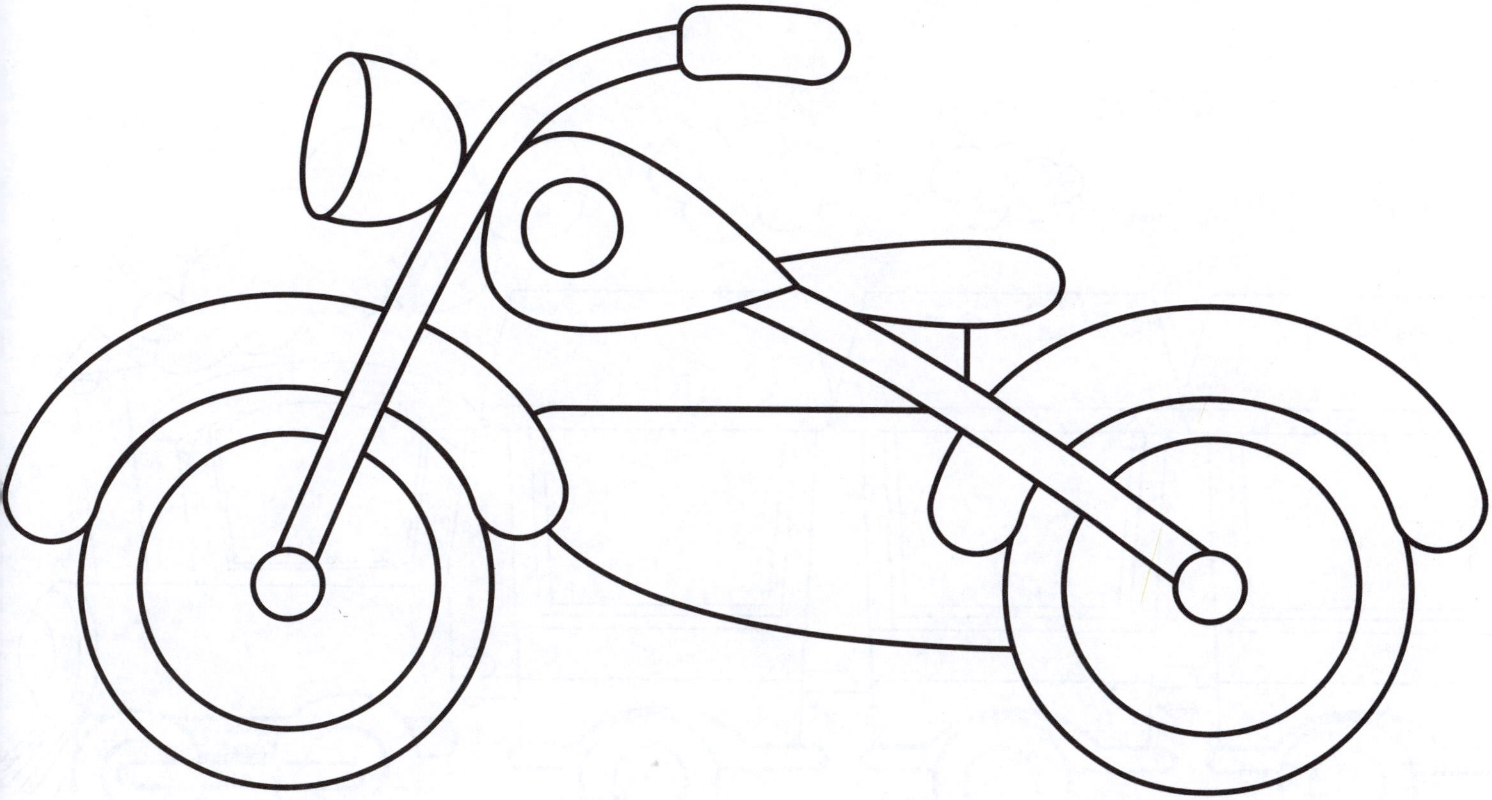

motorbike

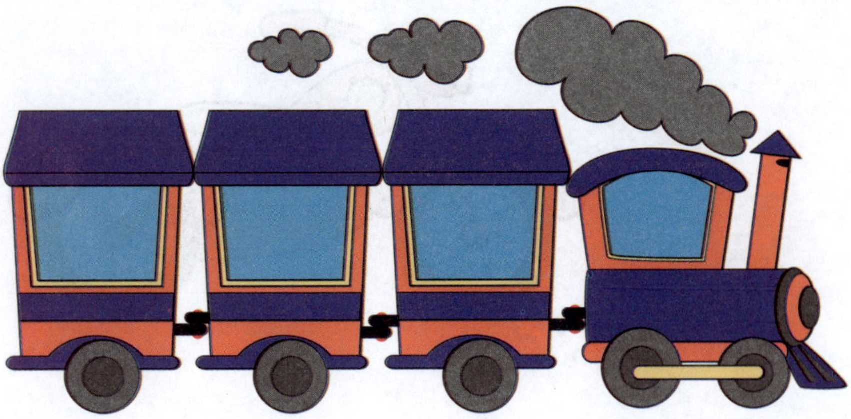

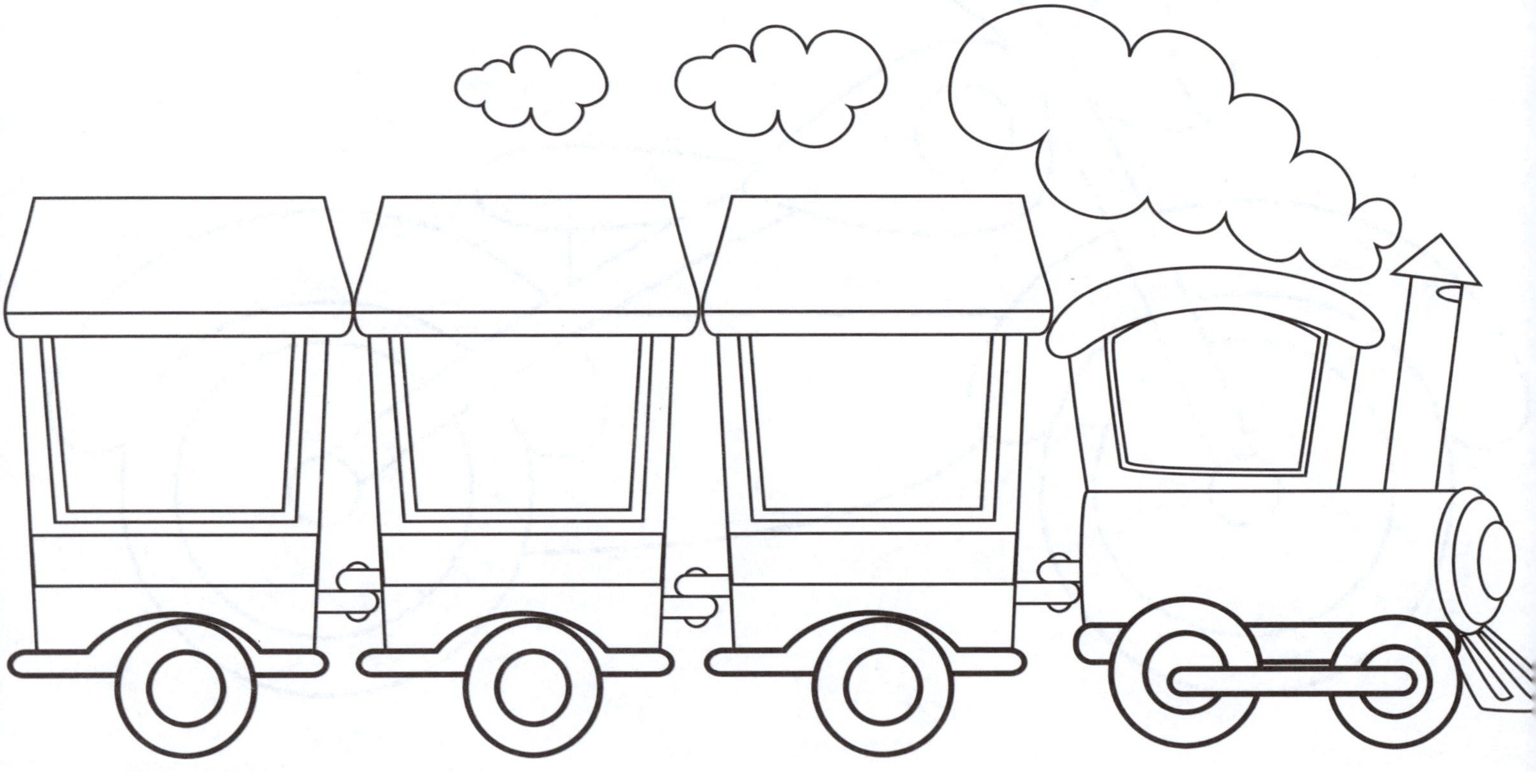

train

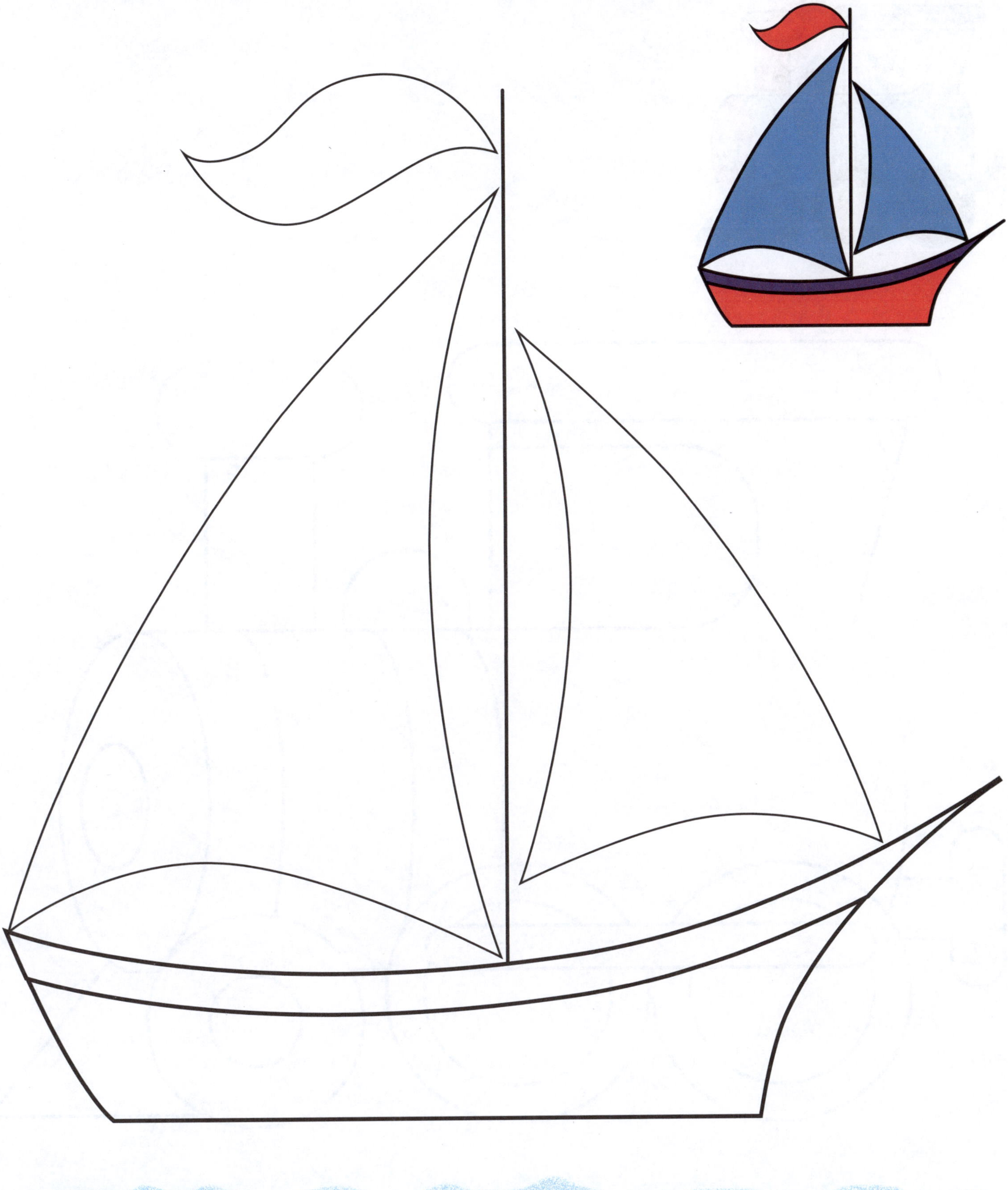

boat

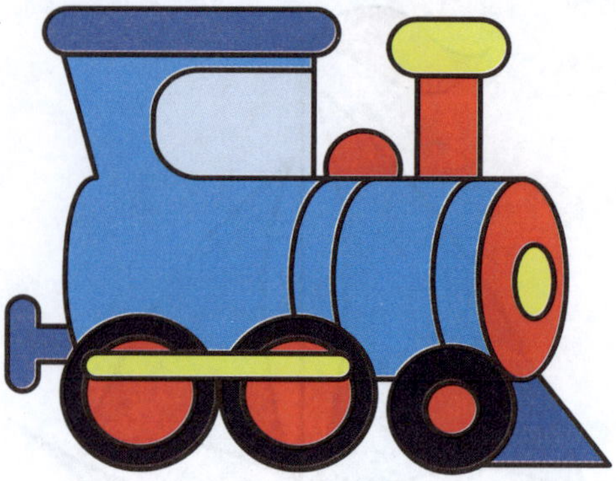

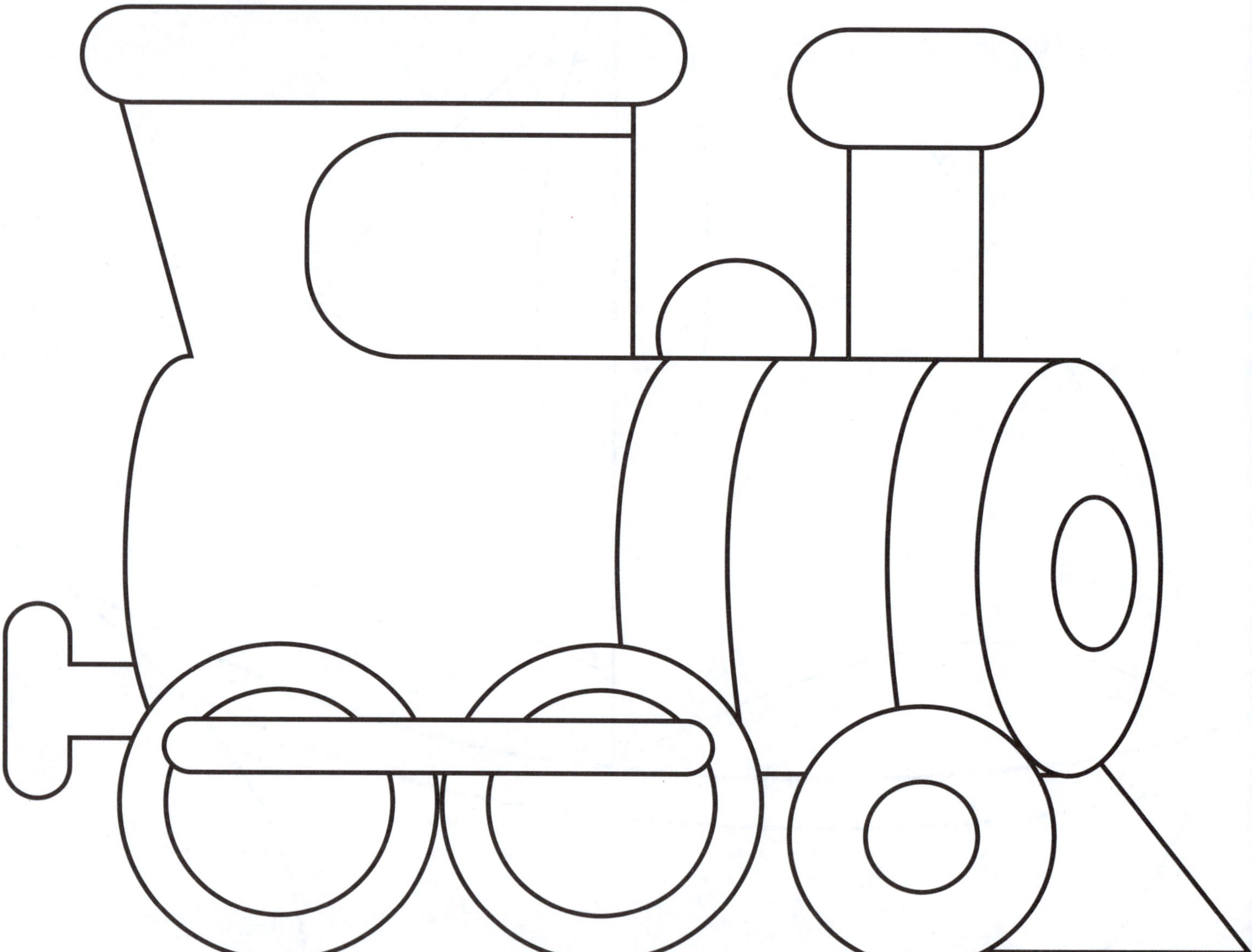

engine

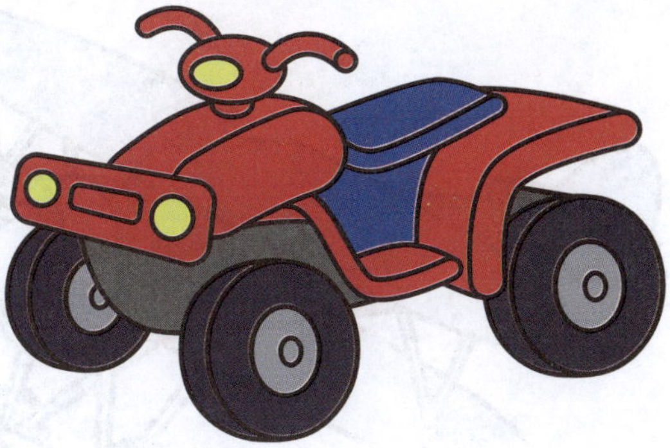

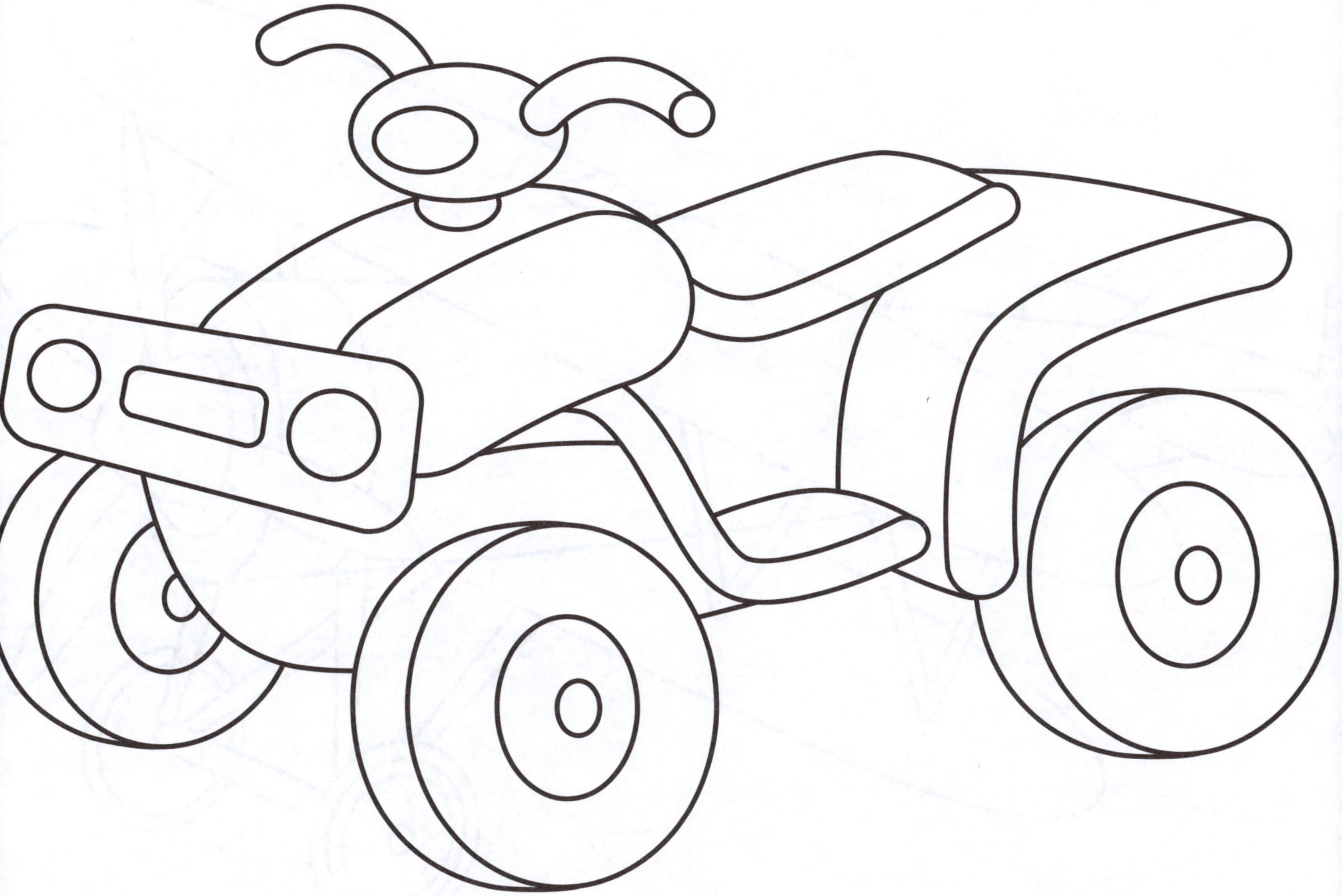

quad bike

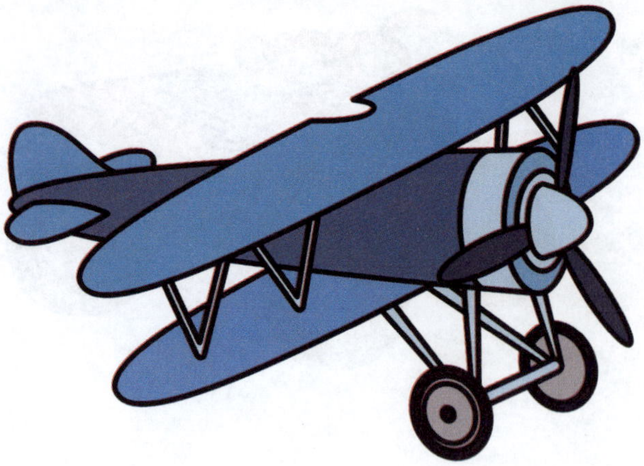

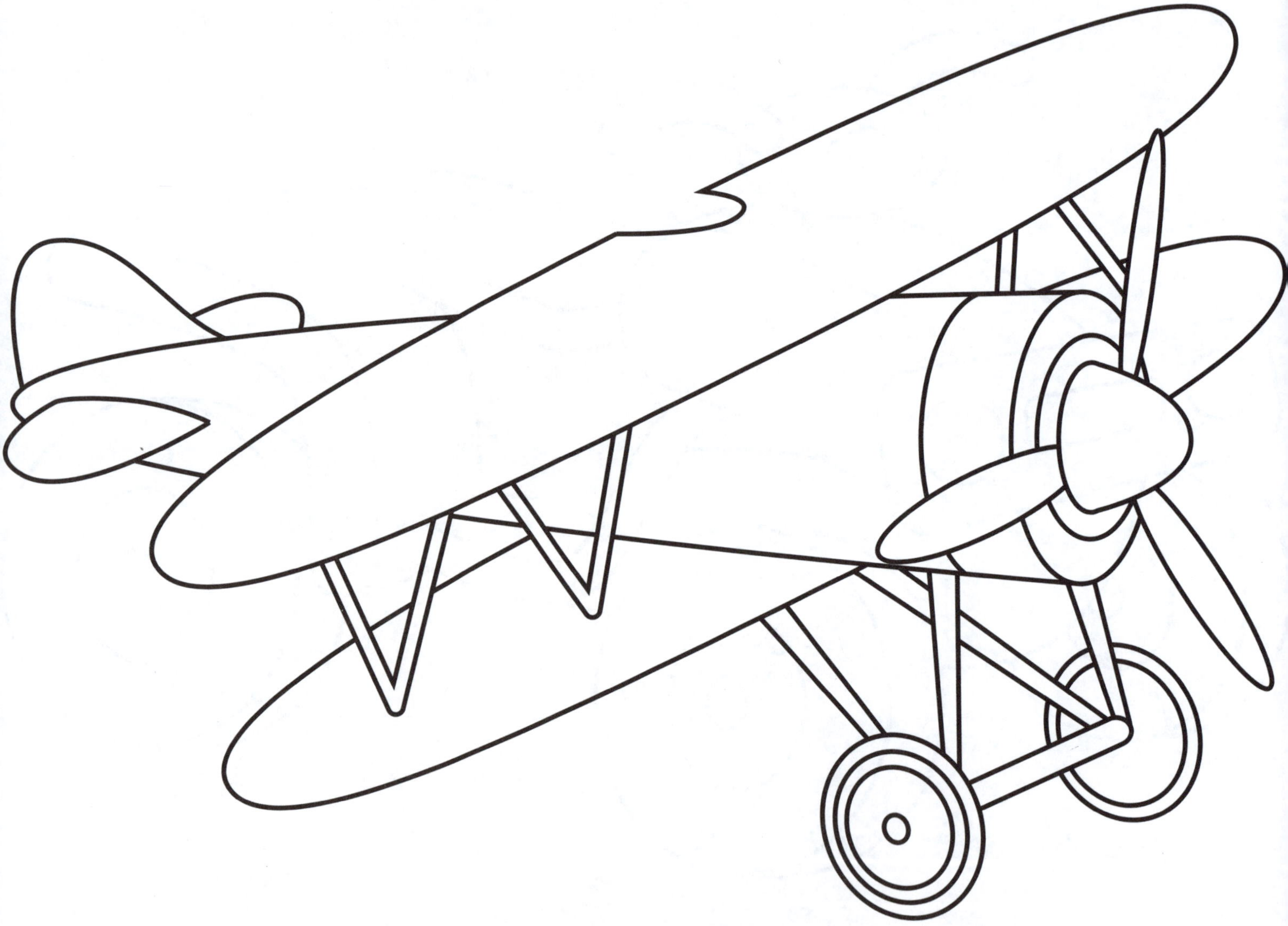

biplane

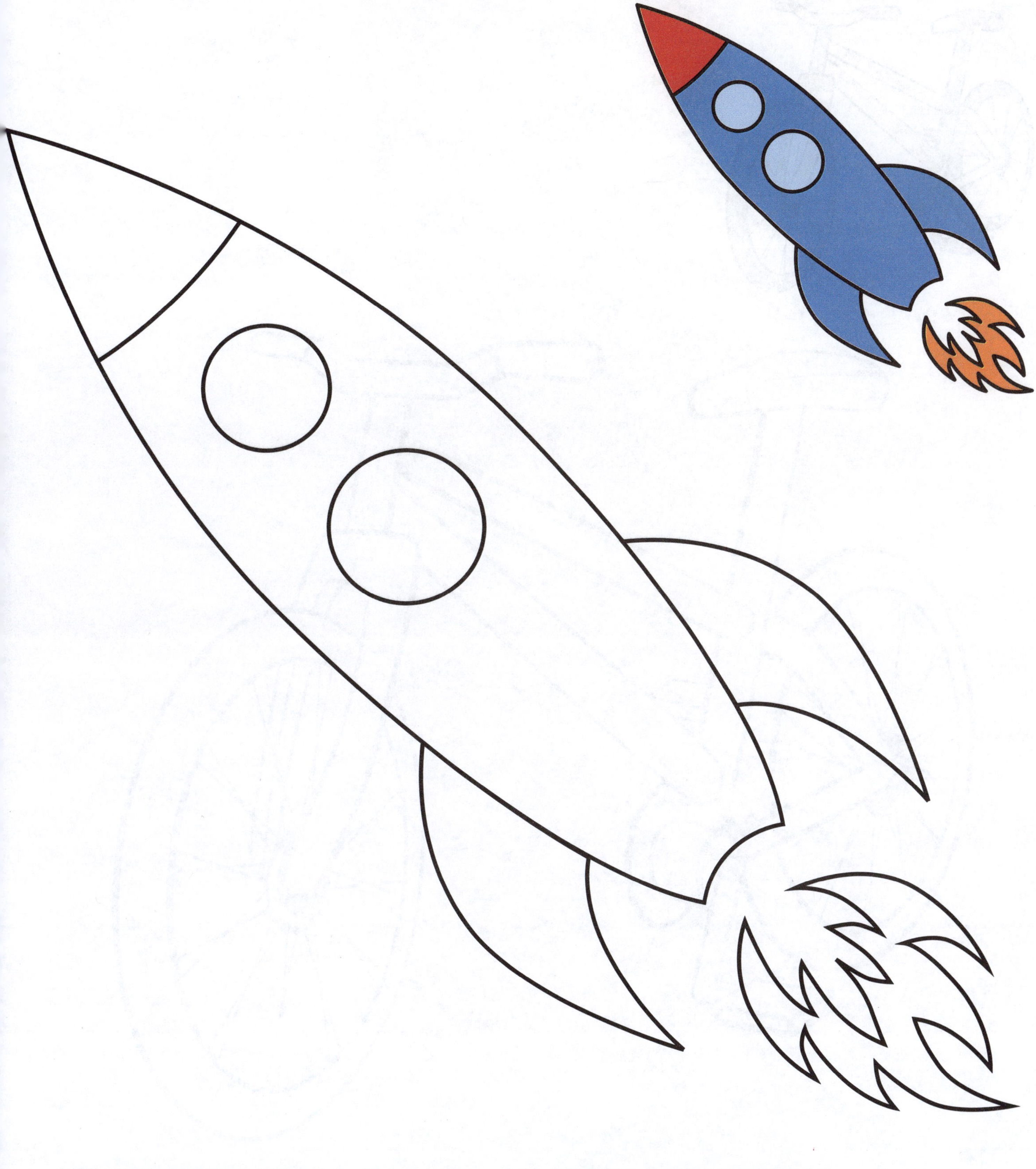

rocket

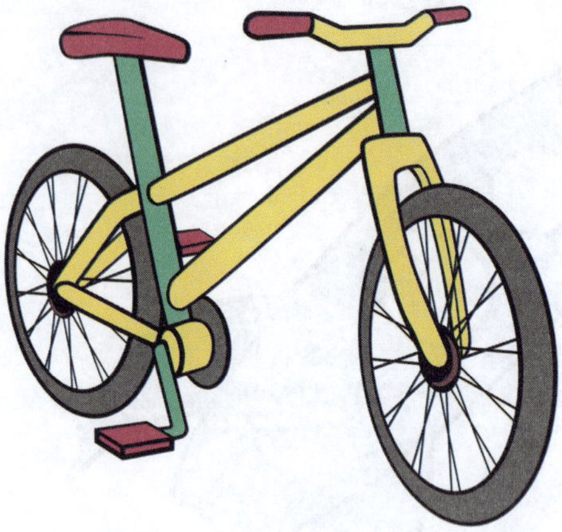

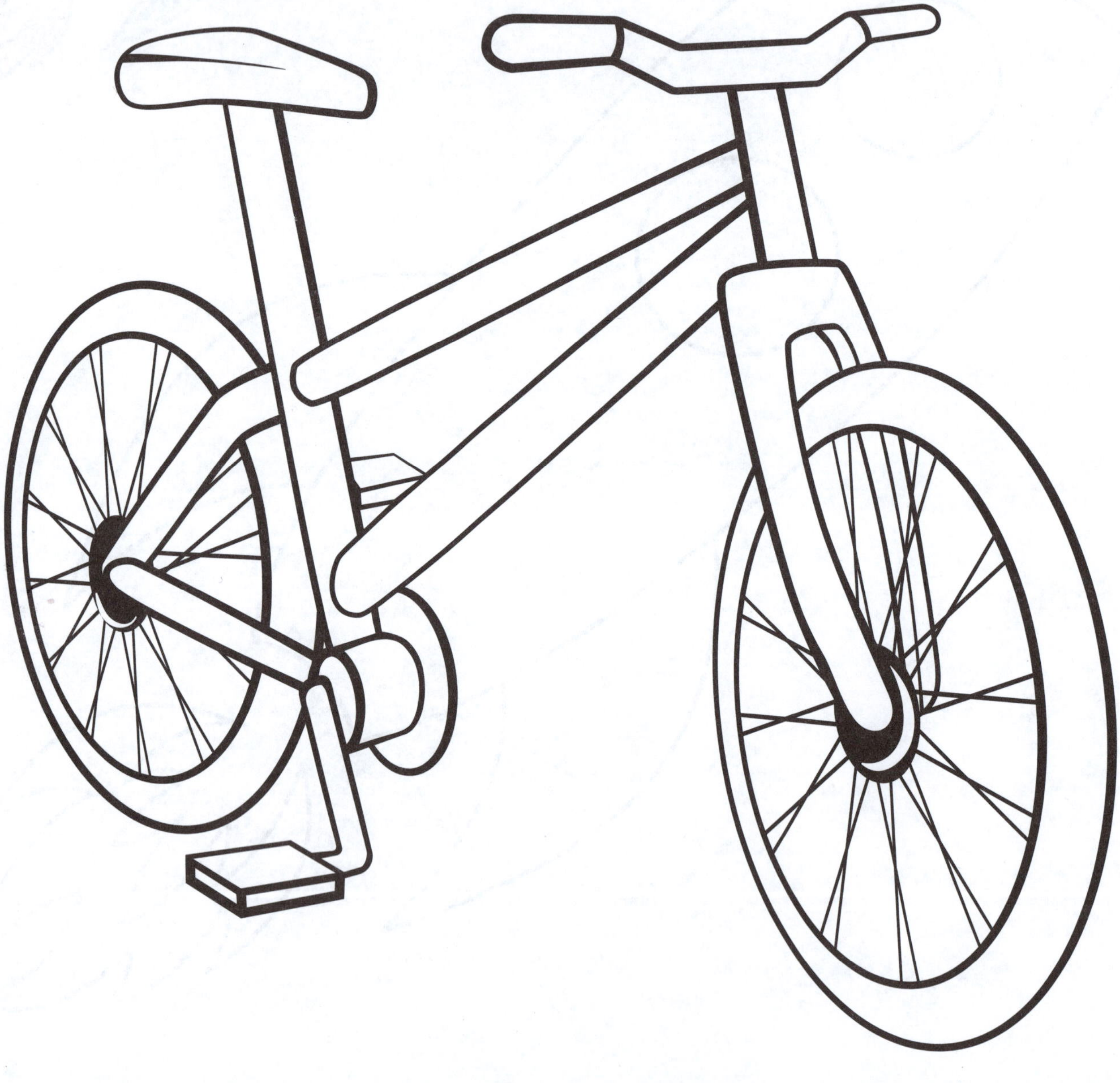

bicycle

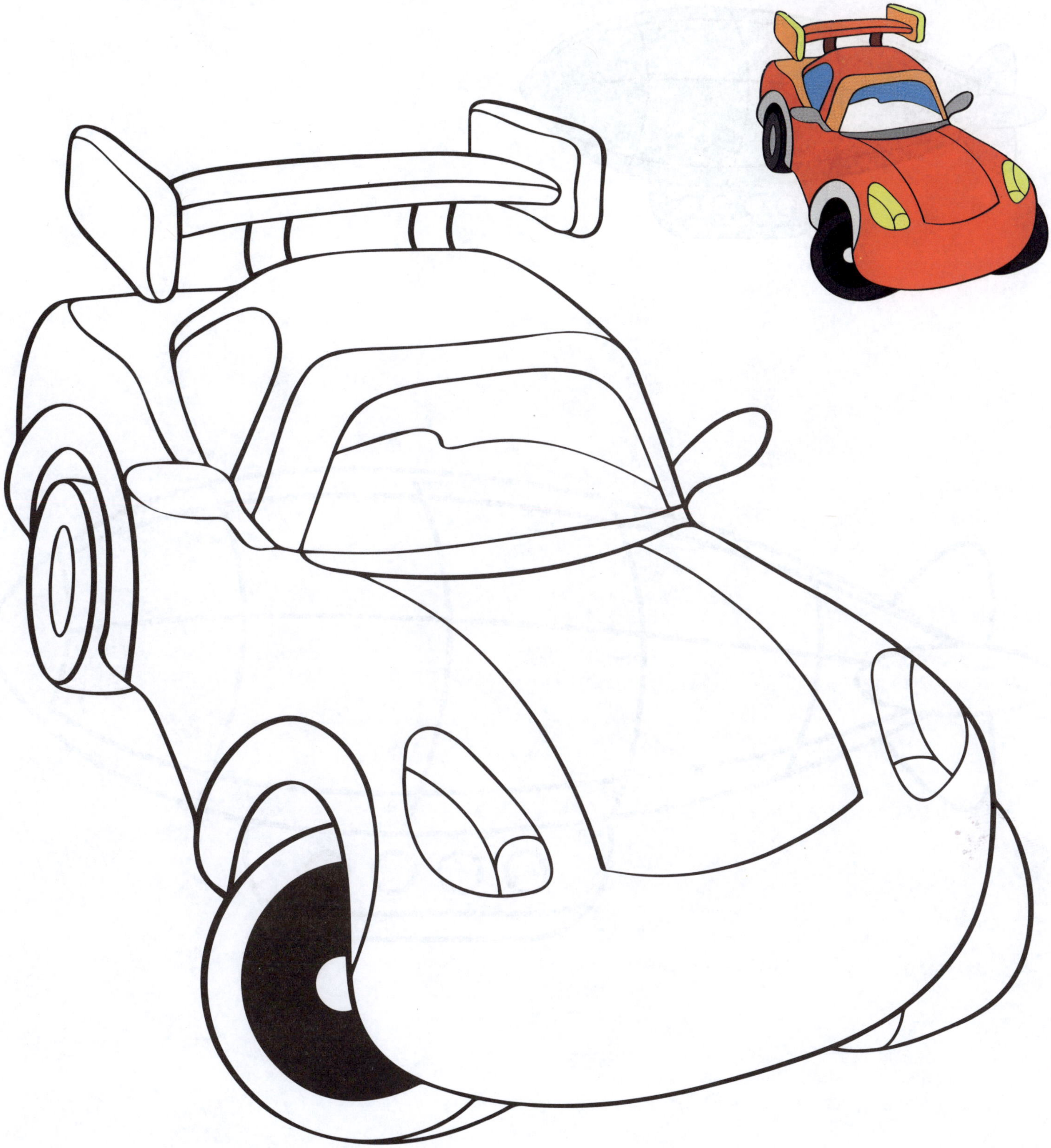

sports car

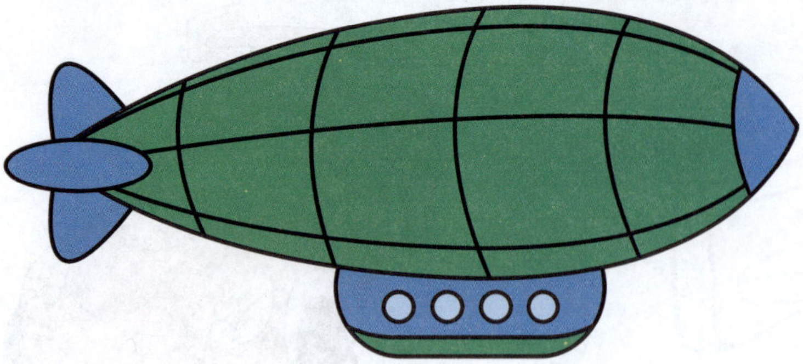

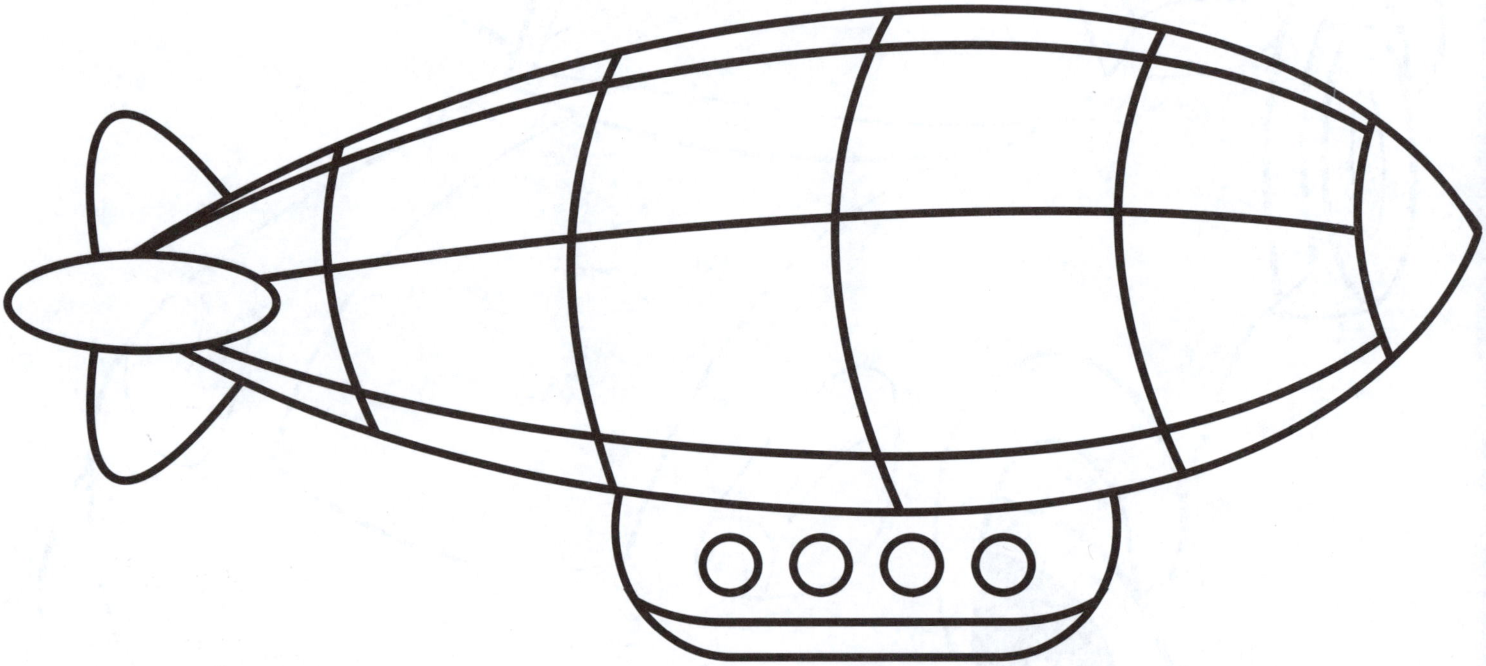

zeppelin